POINTS OF VIEW

I0893123

Should Students Learn About RACISM?

By Layla Owens

KidHaven PUBLISHING

Published in 2023 by
KidHaven Publishing, an Imprint of Greenhaven Publishing, LLC
29 E. 21st Street
New York, NY 10010

Designer: Deanna Paternostro
Editor: Caitie McAneney

Photo credits: Cover GagliardiPhotography/Shutterstock.com; p. 5 LightField Studios/Shuttersrtock.com; p. 7 Gorodenkoff/Shutterstock.com; pp. 9, 21 (inset, left) Tippman98x/Shutterstock.com; p. 11 4 PM production/Shutterstock.com; p. 13 tetiana.photographer/Shutterstock.com; p. 15 Robert Kneschke/Shutterstock.com; p. 17 Pixel-Shot/Shutterstock.com; p. 19 fizkes/Shutterstock.com; p. 21 (notepad) ESB Professional/Shutterstock.com; p. 21 (markers) Kucher Serhii/Shutterstock.com; p. 21 (photo frame) FARBAI/iStock/Thinkstock; p. 21 (inset, middle) Monkey Business Images/Shutterstock.com; p. 21 (inset, right) Rido/Shutterstock.com.

Cataloging-in-Publication Data

Names: Owens, Layla.
Title: Should students learn about racism? / Layla Owens.
Description: New York : KidHaven Publishing, 2023. | Series: Points of view | Includes glossary and index.
Identifiers: ISBN 9781534542051 (pbk.) | ISBN 9781534542075 (library bound) | ISBN 9781534542068 (6pack) | ISBN 9781534542082 (ebook)
Subjects: LCSH: Racism–United States–Juvenile literature. | Debates and debating–Juvenile literature. | United States–Race relations–Juvenile literature.
Classification: LCC E184.A1 O94 2023 | DDC 305.800973–dc23

Printed in the United States of America

Some of the images in this book illustrate individuals who are models. The depictions do not imply actual situations or events.

CPSIA compliance information: Batch #CSKH23: For further information contact Greenhaven Publishing LLC, New York, New York at 1-844-317-7404.

CONTENTS

What Is RACISM?

The United States is a **diverse** country, but throughout U.S. history, white people have held much of the power. Some white Americans enslaved African people, stole land from Native Americans, and **discriminated** against **immigrants**.

Even today, people in America deal with racism. Racism is the practice of treating others unfairly because of their **race**. Some people say that schools should teach about racism to prevent hate and **extremism**. Others say that racism shouldn't be mentioned in schools. You can look at both sides of the argument, as well as the facts, to decide what you think.

Know the Facts!

A 2021 Pew Research survey found that 53 percent of U.S. adults say increased attention to the history of slavery and racism is a good thing for society.

Racism can exist in school, work, neighborhoods, sports teams, health care, and more. It can even describe governments and societies that allow one race to be treated better than others.

Racism in SCHOOLS

You learn about a lot of things in social studies classes. You learn about history, government, and how to be a good citizen. Some people believe that students also need to understand how racism in the United States has shaped public **policies**. This is sometimes called critical race theory (CRT).

The main idea behind critical race theory is that race was invented by society. It claims that racism isn't just about individual people having racial **bias**. It's about a system. They say that racism is woven into today's laws, government systems, and policies. This has a negative, or bad, effect on people of color.

Know the Facts!

States that have banned critical race theory in schools as of 2021 include Texas, Idaho, Oklahoma, and Tennessee.

Many teachers want to be able to show students the full history of the United States—even the parts that are hard, such as slavery.

Teaching the PAST

Many people believe that America's past must be taught as a whole—even the parts that are **violent** or racist. They say that it wouldn't be right to ignore the millions of Black people who were enslaved in the United States—and what they did to help build the country.

Many teachers say that by teaching about all of this, they can help students understand the discrimination Black people still deal with today. This history is very important to much of the population, especially the nearly 47 million U.S. citizens who are Black Americans.

It still affects their lives.

Know the Facts!

The 1860 U.S. **census** showed that nearly 4 million Black people were enslaved in the United States at that time.

Many Black Americans celebrate Juneteenth each year. It's a celebration of the ending of slavery in the United States in 1865.

Punishing White PEOPLE

Some people feel that critical race theory shouldn't be taught in schools because it will make white students feel bad. They think there's no need to teach young people about racism today because it just brings up old issues. It could make divisions between white students and Black students worse.

People who oppose teaching about racist systems in the United States say that it **punishes** white people. It makes white people feel as if they need to make up for something that happened in the past. Some even think that white Americans face discrimination too.

Know the Facts!

A 2017 NPR poll showed that 55 percent of white Americans said they believe white people face discrimination.

Critical race theory can be hard for some white students to learn about.

Anti-Racist WORK

In 2020, **protests** took place across the United States and around the world. Many protests were part of the Black Lives Matter movement. People who attended these protests were upset that a Black man named George Floyd was killed in the United States by a police officer. They called for people to not just be "not racist," but to be "anti-racist."

Anti-racism is actively fighting against racism and calling it out in systems such as schools, health care, and government. Many people believe students should have an anti-racist education to help them grow into good citizens.

Know the Facts!

A 2020 poll from the Southern Poverty Law Center (SPLC) showed that 70 percent of U.S. adults support anti-racist education to reduce and prevent hate and extremism.

Black Lives Matter protests in 2020 called for people to be anti-racist.

Being

COLOR-BLIND

Some people who oppose anti-racism education say that a person's race shouldn't matter. They believe the fight against racism is over. They think that the United States is a fair and free country now and that schools shouldn't give greater attention to racism. They think teaching about it can only cause problems.

Some of these people quote Dr. Martin Luther King Jr., who said that people should not be "judged by the color of their skin, but by the content of their character." Many even claim to "not see color" when they see a person. Therefore, they don't recognize racism as something that still exists.

Know the Facts!

Dr. Martin Luther King Jr. was a leader of the civil rights movement. This was a movement toward equal rights for Black Americans that gained national attention in the 1950s and 1960s.

Some people argue that kids shouldn't be taught about racism because they should be color-blind, or not aware of anyone's race.

Racism TODAY

People who want anti-racist education say that racism isn't a thing of the past—it still exists today. They call it "systemic racism," which means it exists in larger systems in society.

They point to hate crimes against people of color. They talk about how Black Americans are arrested and killed by police at a higher rate than white Americans. They say that there are policies in place to keep Black Americans from voting or buying houses in certain places. These people argue that racism is still alive in America, so it should be taught about in schools.

Know the Facts!

A 2021 Gallup poll found that 64 percent of U.S. adults believe racism is widespread in the United States today.

People say that racism exists in the education system. White students sometimes receive a better education and opportunities than Black students.

Not NECESSARY

Some Americans say that teaching about racism just isn't necessary. They say that the work of fighting racism was done during the American civil rights movement of the 1950s and 1960s. During that time, all Black Americans gained the right to vote and use the same public spaces as white Americans.

The Civil Rights Act of 1964 **prohibits** discrimination on the basis of race, color, religion, sex, or where a person comes from. Some people say that this law did everything necessary to stop discrimination. They don't think people have to actively work against racism anymore.

Know the Facts!

The Voting Rights Act of 1965 made it illegal to keep someone from voting because of their race throughout the United States.

Some people say that Black people have all the opportunities they need to have a good life in the United States.

Diversity in AMERICA

Racism is nothing new in the United States. Racism was written into the history of the United States from its earliest days—long before it even became a country. However, people differ in their points of view about teaching this part of the past—and present—to kids.

Some people say that teaching about racism today would just make more divisions between people. It would make white students feel bad. Other people say that the discomfort of white students shouldn't outweigh the needs of Black students. They say it's wrong to limit what teachers can teach about history. As a student, what do you think?

Know the Facts!

In 1980, 80 percent of Americans were white. In 2020, about 60 percent of Americans were white. This shows the country is becoming more diverse.

Should students learn about racism?

YES

- Racism played a major part in U.S. history.
- Anti-racist education policies are an important part of teaching kids to be good citizens.
- Racism is still alive in American systems and laws.
- It's wrong to limit what teachers can teach about diversity and racism.

NO

- White Americans today shouldn't be punished for racism in the past.
- Schools shouldn't point out differences in race.
- Racism doesn't exist anymore, so teaching about it is unnecessary.
- Teaching about racism today would make white students feel uncomfortable.

You can look at all sides of a topic, then use facts and your experience to inform your own point of view.

GLOSSARY

bias: A personal and sometimes unreasoned judgement against someone or something for some reason, such as race.

census: A counting of the population done by the government.

discriminate: To treat people unequally based on class, race, or religion.

diverse: Having many different types, forms, or ideas.

extremism: Promoting harmful, extreme measures or views.

immigrant: A person who comes to a country to live there.

policy: A set of rules for how something is to be done.

prohibit: To keep someone from doing something.

protest: An event at which people speak out about something. Also, to speak out strongly against something.

punish: To make someone suffer for doing something wrong.

race: A group of people from the same part of the world that share some physical characteristics.

violent: Relating to the use of force to hurt others.

For More INFORMATION

WEBSITES

Dealing with Bullies
kidshealth.org/en/kids/bullies.html#catemotion
Sometimes students are bullied at school for their race. Learn how to deal with bullying through this website.

Talk About Race and Racism
pbskids.org/video/dots-spot/3047127185
Watch this video about race and racism by PBS Kids.

BOOKS

Lacy, Jane. *Racism*. New York, NY: Rosen Publishing, 2019.

McAneney, Caitie. *What Do I Do When People I Know Are Racist?* New York, NY: PowerKids Press, 2020.

Saidian, Siyavush. *Did the Civil Rights Movement Achieve Civil Rights?* New York, NY: PowerKids Press, 2019.

INDEX